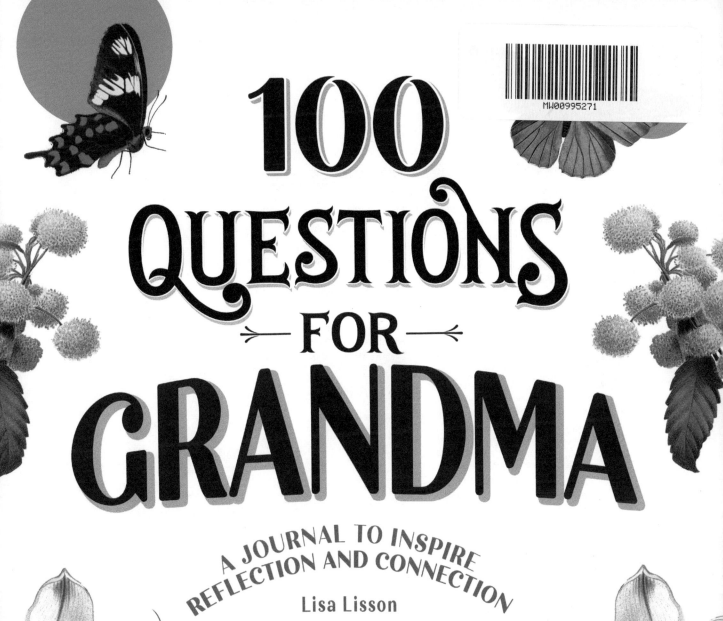

100 QUESTIONS

≫ FOR ≪

GRANDMA

A JOURNAL TO INSPIRE REFLECTION AND CONNECTION

Lisa Lisson

ROCKRIDGE
PRESS

First Rockridge Press trade paperback and hardcover edition 2022

Rockridge Press and the Rockridge Press logo are trademarks or registered trademarks of Callisto Media Inc. and/or its affiliates in the United States and other countries and may not be used without written permission.

For general information on our other products and services, please contact our Customer Care Department within the United States at (866) 744-2665, or outside the United States at (510) 253-0500.

Hardcover ISBN: 979-8-88608-134-3
Paperback ISBN: 979-8-88608-829-8

Manufactured in the United States of America

Interior and Cover Designer: Tricia Jang
Art Producer: Hannah Dickerson
Editor: Kahlil Thomas
Production Editor: Ashley Polikoff
Production Manager: Martin Worthington

All illustrations used under license from Digital Curio/Creative Market, BlackBird Foundry/Creative Market and Artist's Archive/Creative Market. Author photo courtesy of Erika Dietrick.

10 9 8 7 6 5 4 3 2 1 0

THIS JOURNAL BELONGS TO

_____

CONTENTS

INTRODUCTION

I grew up going to family reunions and family holiday dinners of all sizes and listening to the stories told by my family's older generations. These stories held our family's history and the life lessons and wisdom of those generations. Unfortunately, as a young person I paid little attention to them and remembered only a few. Luckily, as an adult my interest in researching my own genealogy began. I soon recognized the valuable information in those family stories and memories.

As a genealogy researcher and writer, I have spent countless hours seeking out and interviewing my family members for their unique stories and life lessons. I was able to interview my paternal grandmother multiple times during her final years. She answered all my questions, which allowed me to understand and know her on a much deeper level. I got tips for the "famous cornbread" recipe and learned why she did not like to drive. I also learned about her love of travel and identified with her desire to travel more. Her stories are precious memories.

Throughout the interviews with my family members, the importance of documenting and telling my own story became clear. It is easy in the busyness of family life to overlook our own unique stories, but I'm here to tell you that your stories and history are important. They bridge the generations that came before and will come after you, and yet it's likely that your history has yet to be recorded or written down.

100 Questions for Grandma: A Journal to Inspire Reflection and Connection gives you an opportunity to join your family's history before it's too late. It was created to help you keep your stories alive, giving current and future generations the opportunity to connect with their past and identify with their family history. It may be that your upbringing was nontraditional or you know little, if any, information about your family's origins. Perhaps you were not biologically related to your identified family. All of that is perfectly fine. This is your story.

As you sit down to record your answers to the prompts, take your time. There are no right or wrong answers. The prompts will ask you to reflect and write on your early years, love and friendship, your passions, and your feelings on becoming a grandmother. Share what you want your grandchildren and future generations to know about your life.

This journal is your story in your own words.
Enjoy the opportunity to reflect on your life.
Share your answers with your grandchildren and
enjoy developing your relationships even more!

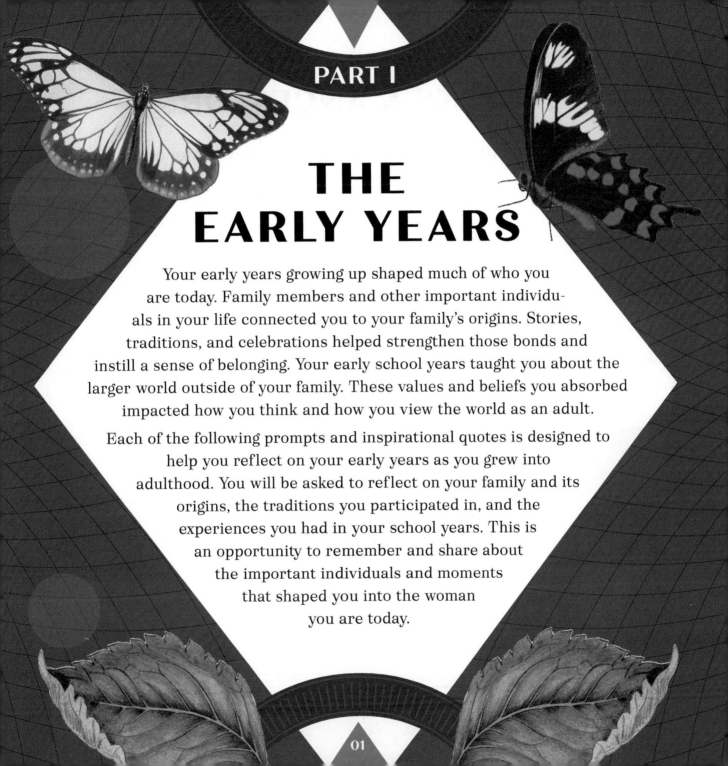

PART I

THE EARLY YEARS

Your early years growing up shaped much of who you are today. Family members and other important individuals in your life connected you to your family's origins. Stories, traditions, and celebrations helped strengthen those bonds and instill a sense of belonging. Your early school years taught you about the larger world outside of your family. These values and beliefs you absorbed impacted how you think and how you view the world as an adult.

Each of the following prompts and inspirational quotes is designed to help you reflect on your early years as you grew into adulthood. You will be asked to reflect on your family and its origins, the traditions you participated in, and the experiences you had in your school years. This is an opportunity to remember and share about the important individuals and moments that shaped you into the woman you are today.

ORIGINS & ANCESTORS

What is your full name? Were you named after someone? If so, who were they?

_____

_____

_____

_____

_____

_____

_____

_____

_____

_____

Where did your ancestors originate? Has your family been present in your current location for generations, or are they recent immigrants? Share any family stories about your family's origins.

_____

_____

_____

_____

_____

_____

_____

_____

_____

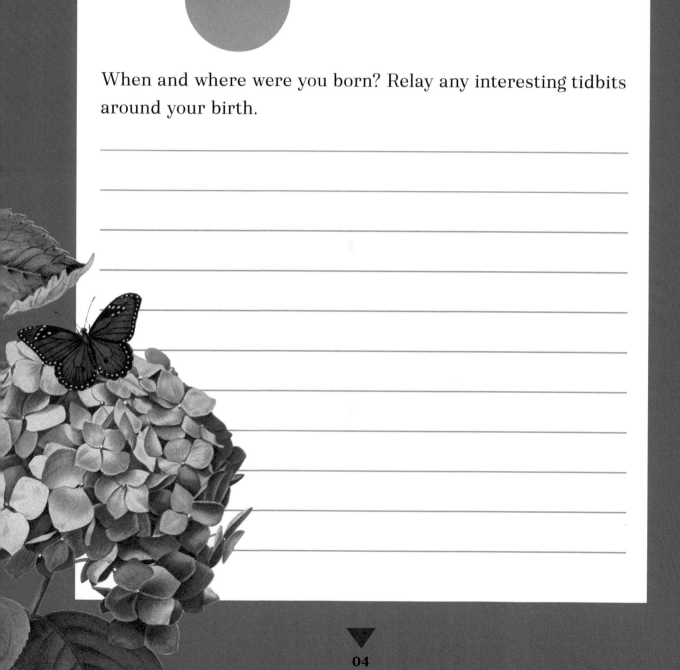

When and where were you born? Relay any interesting tidbits around your birth.

Where did you grow up? How many times did you move prior to becoming an adult?

_____

_____

_____

_____

_____

_____

_____

_____

_____

_____

Describe the home where you grew up. Was it a house, apartment, or something else? Who lived there with you?

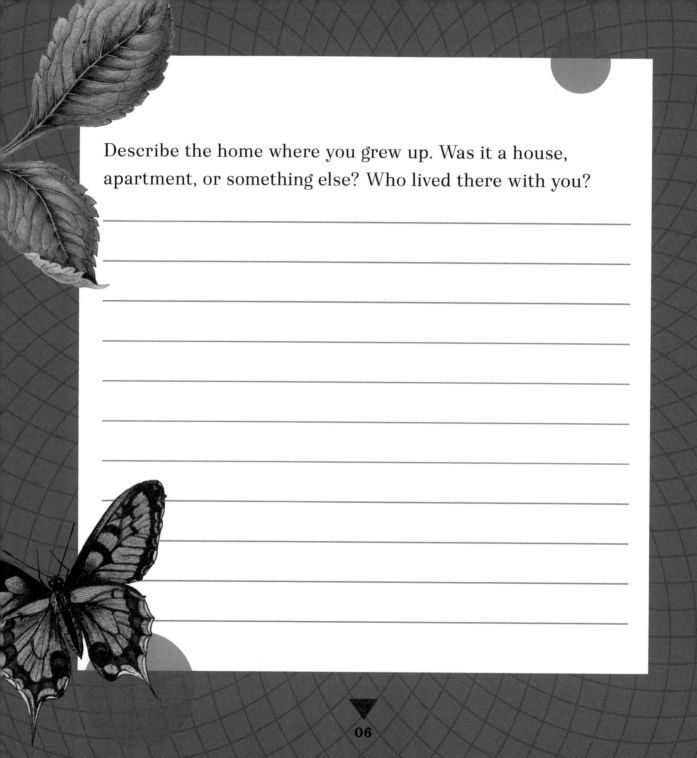

"

All of our **ANCESTORS LIVE WITHIN EACH ONE OF US** whether we are aware of it or not.

"

LAURENCE OVERMIRE

FAMILY

What are the full names of your parents or guardians? If applicable, do you know the story of how they met?

_____

_____

_____

_____

_____

_____

_____

_____

_____

_____

Think about your parents' or guardians' personalities.
Describe them, if possible.

_____

_____

_____

_____

_____

_____

_____

_____

_____

Sibling relationships are special. Do you have any siblings? If so, what are their full names and what is the birth order?

_____

_____

_____

_____

_____

_____

_____

_____

Who were your favorite relatives or family friends growing up? What qualities about the relationships made them your favorite?

_____

_____

_____

_____

_____

_____

_____

_____

_____

Did you see relatives on a regular basis? If so, which ones?
Did they live close to you or far away?

_____

_____

_____

_____

_____

_____

_____

_____

_____

Your story **IS WHAT YOU HAVE,** what you will **ALWAYS HAVE.** It is something to own.

MICHELLE OBAMA

TRADITIONS

Did you celebrate any holidays or special occasions when you were growing up? Describe the food and activities of those special times.

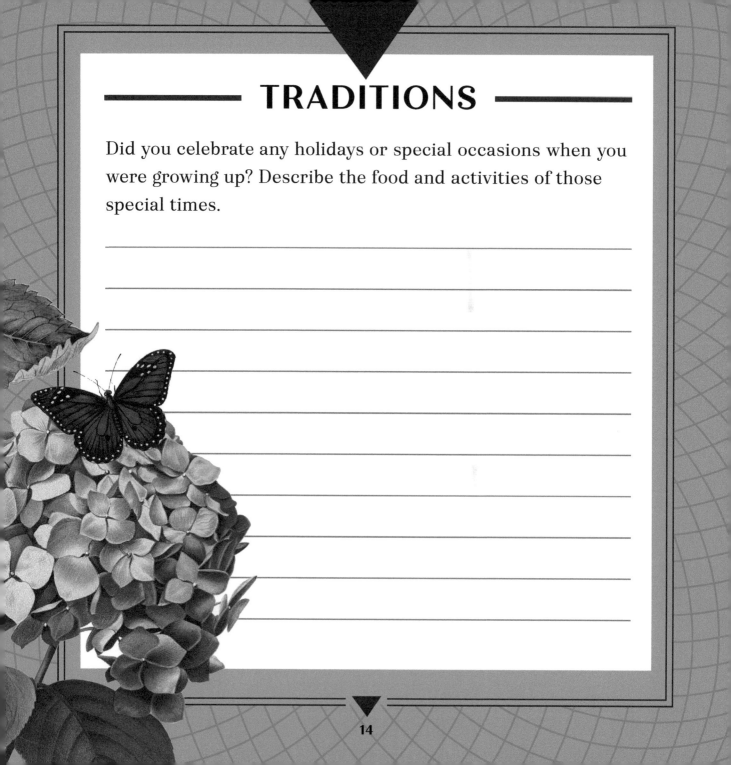

_____

_____

_____

_____

_____

_____

_____

_____

_____

Birthdays can be anticipated events for children and adults alike. How did you your family celebrate your birthday when you were a child? Describe a memorable birthday celebration.

_____

_____

_____

_____

_____

_____

_____

_____

Family traditions are unique and can range from large parties to small gatherings. They may sometimes include quirky customs. Describe your favorite family traditions from when you were growing up.

_____

_____

_____

_____

_____

_____

_____

_____

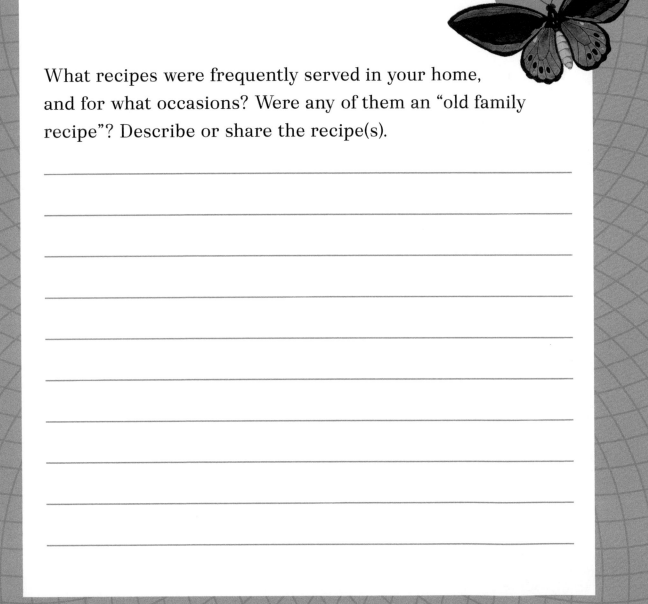

What recipes were frequently served in your home, and for what occasions? Were any of them an "old family recipe"? Describe or share the recipe(s).

_____

_____

_____

_____

_____

_____

_____

_____

_____

What new family traditions have you created in your own family? Describe a tradition you enjoy sharing with your grandchildren.

_____

_____

_____

_____

_____

_____

_____

_____

A people without the
knowledge of their
PAST HISTORY,
ORIGIN,
AND CULTURE
is like a tree
without roots.

MARCUS GARVEY

SCHOOLING

What was the first day of school like for you? Were you excited or nervous? Describe your first day of school and your favorite activities at school.

_____

_____

_____

_____

_____

_____

_____

_____

_____

_____

Thinking back over your school years, is there one memory that stands out? Describe that memory and the impact it had on you.

What was your favorite subject in school? Why was it your favorite? Did you end up pursuing a career around that interest?

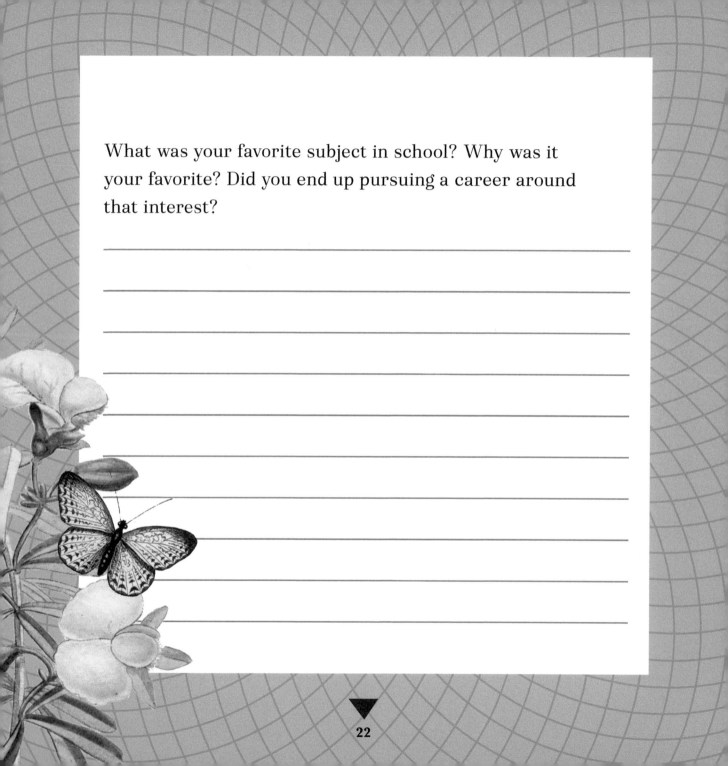

What types of sports or clubs did you participate in during your school years? Do you continue to have those interests today?

_____

_____

_____

_____

_____

_____

_____

_____

_____

What was your course of study, and what drew you to it? Did you learn in a formal setting or was it through self-learning?

_____

_____

_____

_____

_____

_____

_____

_____

_____

EDUCATION
is the key to
unlocking the world,
A PASSPORT
TO FREEDOM.

OPRAH WINFREY

PART II

PASSIONS & PURSUITS

The pursuit of your passions and dreams is intensely personal. You might have chosen your career based on your passion. Your passions might have led you to participate in a particular civic cause or an enjoyable hobby. Consider how your dreams impacted your life decisions or were driven by your values. Do not overlook the nostalgic places in your life. Explore why they evoke that feeling. Each of the following prompts and inspirational quotes is designed to help you reflect on the pursuit of your passions and dreams, your life's work, and the things that are meaningful to you regardless of reason. You will be reflecting on some of your favorite things, your interests, your values, and those places and things you remember fondly.

Take this opportunity to share with your grandchildren the stories and things that brought meaning and enjoyment to your life.

A FEW FAVORITES

What specific activity adds joy to your day? What aspect of this activity brings you so much enjoyment?

_____

_____

_____

_____

_____

_____

_____

_____

_____

What hobbies do you enjoy? Have you always enjoyed
these activities? What do you like about your hobbies?

_____

_____

_____

_____

_____

_____

_____

_____

_____

_____

What was your favorite toy as a child? Was it a gift from someone special or one you bought on your own?

_____

_____

_____

_____

_____

_____

_____

_____

_____

Music comes in many styles. What type of music do you enjoy? Share your favorite piece of music or favorite artist.

_____

_____

_____

_____

_____

_____

_____

_____

_____

What types of books do you enjoy reading? Do you have a favorite book that you have read more than once? What draws you to it?

We do not
remember days,
**WE
REMEMBER
MOMENTS.**

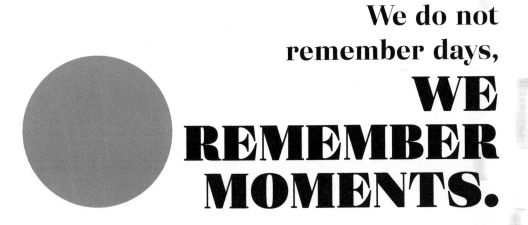

CESARE PAVESE

—JOBS & OTHER INTERESTS—

What was your first job? Was it a part-time summer job or full-time employment? What were your responsibilities?

_____

_____

_____

_____

_____

_____

_____

_____

_____

_____

Describe a lifelong interest or project. What parts of it do you find particularly interesting?

_____

_____

_____

_____

_____

_____

_____

_____

_____

_____

_____

What type of career did or do you have? What was it about it that interested you?

_____

_____

_____

_____

_____

_____

_____

_____

_____

_____

_____

What important life skills or life lessons have you learned through your work?

_____

_____

_____

_____

_____

_____

_____

_____

_____

_____

Reflect on the opportunities you have been offered in your education or career. Describe a missed opportunity. If it were presented again, would you make the same decision?

_____

_____

_____

_____

_____

_____

_____

_____

_____

_____

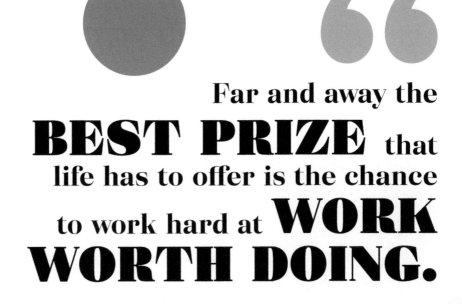

Far and away the **BEST PRIZE** that life has to offer is the chance to work hard at **WORK WORTH DOING.**

THEODORE ROOSEVELT

VALUES & BELIEFS

Beliefs and values are passed from one generation to the next.
What core beliefs or traits did your family value?

_____

_____

_____

_____

_____

_____

_____

_____

_____

_____

_____

How did your values define you and dictate how to lead your life? Share the value that guides your life decisions the most.

_____

_____

_____

_____

_____

_____

_____

_____

_____

_____

What role did spirituality play in your life? Describe your basic beliefs and how they guide your way of life.

_____

_____

_____

_____

_____

_____

_____

_____

_____

How did you choose to participate in your community? Were you a member of an organization's board or did you participate in local politics?

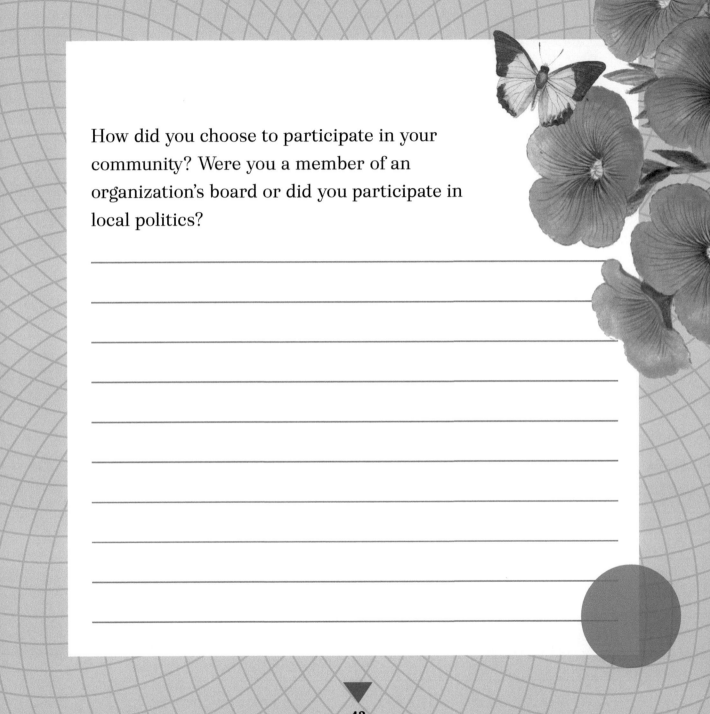

_____

_____

_____

_____

_____

_____

_____

_____

What is the best advice you ever received? Who gave it to you? What impact did the advice have on your life?

_____

_____

_____

_____

_____

_____

_____

_____

_____

_____

"

I've learned that people will forget
what you said, people will forget
what you did, but people will
never forget

HOW YOU MADE
THEM FEEL.

"

MAYA ANGELOU

NOSTALGIC PLACES & THINGS

Describe the neighborhood where you grew up. Who lived near you? Did you know your neighbors?

_____

_____

_____

_____

_____

_____

_____

_____

_____

_____

What family heirlooms or keepsakes do you have and cherish? Who did you get them from? Describe them.

_____

_____

_____

_____

_____

_____

_____

_____

_____

_____

Do you have many family photographs? What photograph means the most to you? Why is it important to you? Share the story behind the photograph.

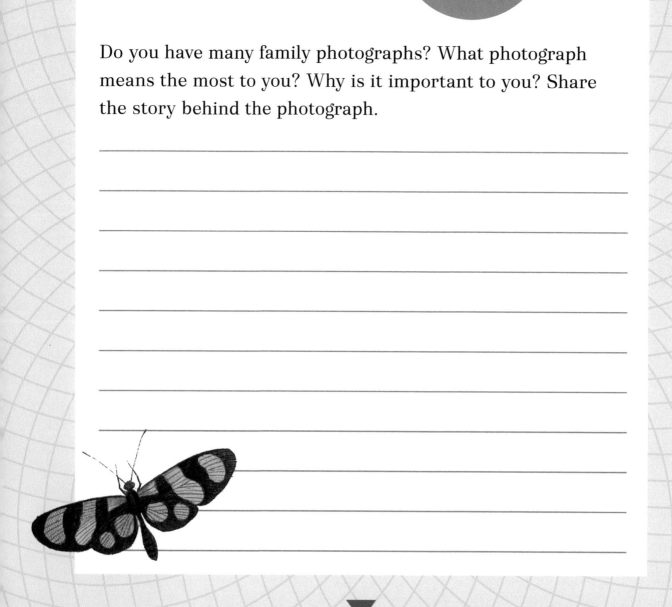

What were your favorite summertime memories as a child? With whom and how did you spend your time?

_____

_____

_____

_____

_____

_____

_____

_____

_____

_____

Did you have a special place where you spent time and found comfort while growing up? Was it a specific chair at home or maybe a spot at a local park? Share what drew you to that spot.

" STORIES NEVER LIVE ALONE:

They are the branches
of a family that we have to trace
back, and forward. "

ROBERTO CALASSO

PART III

LOVE & FRIENDSHIP

Love and friendship bring immense joy to life. You start to build friendships from an early age. Some may last for a short time, whereas others can last an entire lifetime. Through these relationships, you can be inspired, learn about the world through another's eyes, find support in the tough times, and share adventures in the fun times.

Romantic relationships also bring happiness and fulfillment. Everyone's course through romantic love is different. The qualities you look for in a partner are unique to you as an individual. Your personal journey may have included many romantic relationships or a love-at-first-sight experience.

In this section you will find prompts and inspirational quotes to help you reflect on your big firsts and your friendships, mentorships, and romantic relationships.

BIG FIRSTS

How old were you when you learned to ride a bike? Describe your experience and feelings of accomplishment.

_____

_____

_____

_____

_____

_____

_____

_____

_____

_____

What was your experience living away from your childhood home for the first time? Was it when you went to college, got a new job, got married, or something else?

_____

_____

_____

_____

_____

_____

_____

_____

_____

Describe the time when you realized you were no longer a kid. Was it driving a car for the first time, starting your first job, or something else?

_____

_____

_____

_____

_____

_____

_____

_____

_____

_____

A first kiss can be a very memorable occasion. Share the story of your first kiss. Who did you share it with? Where did it happen?

_____

_____

_____

_____

_____

_____

_____

_____

_____

Casting your first vote is an exciting event! How did you feel being able to participate in an election for the first time?

_____

_____

_____

_____

_____

_____

_____

_____

_____

_____

" Be **BRAVE,** Be **CURIOUS,** Be **DETERMINED,** overcome the odds. It can be done. "

STEPHEN HAWKING

FRIENDSHIP

Growing up, who was your best friend? How did you meet, and what things did you do together?

_____

_____

_____

_____

_____

_____

_____

_____

_____

_____

_____

Describe a typical outing spent with family or close friends.
Relate a fun story from your time together.

_____

_____

_____

_____

_____

_____

_____

_____

_____

_____

Who is that one friend you call to share everything with? How did you meet and become friends in the first place?

What is the most fun you have ever experienced with a friend? What were you doing? Where was it? Was it spontaneous, or did you plan it?

_____

_____

_____

_____

_____

_____

_____

_____

_____

_____

What qualities do you value in your friendships? Trustworthiness? Loyalty? Spontaneity? Why are these qualities important to you?

" As soon as he saw the Big Boots, Pooh knew that an

ADVENTURE WAS GOING TO HAPPEN "

A. A. MILNE

ROMANTIC RELATIONSHIPS

Share the story of how you met your partner or spouse. Was it by chance? What was the first thing you noticed about them?

_____

_____

_____

_____

_____

_____

_____

_____

_____

Share a memory of a cherished time or experience you had with your partner or spouse.

_____

_____

_____

_____

_____

_____

_____

_____

_____

_____

Who was your first love? What drew you to that person?

Did you date often? When you dated, what qualities were you looking for in a potential partner?

_____

_____

_____

_____

_____

_____

_____

_____

_____

_____

_____

What hardships have you and your spouse or partner endured in your relationship? How did you overcome them?

_____

_____

_____

_____

_____

_____

_____

_____

_____

_____

For the two of us,
home isn't a place.
It's a person.

AND WE'RE
FINALLY HOME.

STEPHANIE PERKINS

MENTORS & INSPIRATIONAL PEOPLE

Growing up, who in your family did you admire and look up to? Which of their qualities did you adopt as your own?

_____

_____

_____

_____

_____

_____

_____

_____

What teacher influenced you the most during your school years? Reflect on that influence and how it impacted your life.

_____

_____

_____

_____

_____

_____

_____

_____

_____

_____

Who or what were you obsessed with as a teen? Was it a celebrity or a musical group? Did you ever see them in person?

_____

_____

_____

_____

_____

_____

_____

_____

_____

During your career, who influenced you the most? Did they teach you a specific skill? How did learning that skill affect your job?

_____

_____

_____

_____

_____

_____

_____

_____

_____

Have you been a mentor to anyone in your life? Which of your qualities or values did or do you hope to inspire in them?

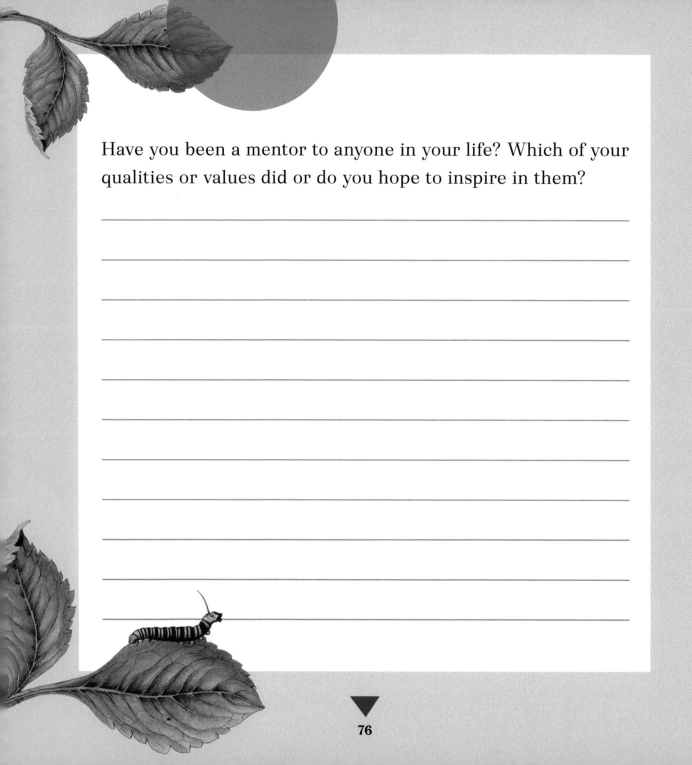

"
Alone we can
do so little;
TOGETHER
WE CAN DO
SO MUCH.
"
HELEN KELLER

PART IV

ON BEING A GRANDMOTHER

Becoming a grandmother for the first time is a joyous occasion. As you welcomed your sweet grandchild into the world, you also welcomed the beginning of your family's next generation. You might have searched their features to see who in the family they looked like. As your grandchild grew, you may have caught glimpses of your own personality in them.

When you became a grandmother, you likely found yourself thinking back on your own experiences as a first-time mother. You may have found yourself remembering the joy of celebrating your child's milestones. You also likely remembered the challenges of motherhood.

Each of the following prompts and inspirational quotes is designed to help you reflect on your thoughts and feelings on becoming a grandmother for the first time.

MOTHERHOOD

Becoming a mother is a special experience. Describe your feelings as you anticipated becoming and then became a mother for the very first time.

What are the full names of your children? Share the stories behind choosing their names.

_____

_____

_____

_____

_____

_____

_____

_____

_____

_____

Each child is an individual. What unique qualities did your children exhibit? Were they ones they shared with you?

_____

_____

_____

_____

_____

_____

_____

_____

_____

What was the most challenging aspect of motherhood for you? How did you meet that challenge?

Mothers teach their children many things–such as patience and perseverance. In the same way, children can teach their mothers many things. What lessons did you learn from your children during their growing-up years?

_____

_____

_____

_____

_____

_____

_____

_____

If I were asked to define

MOTHERHOOD.

I would have defined it as

LOVE IN ITS PUREST FORM. UNCONDITIONAL LOVE.

REVATHI SANKARAN

MILESTONES

A child starting school is a big moment. What was the first day of school like for your children? What were your feelings as they entered the classroom?

_____

_____

_____

_____

_____

_____

_____

_____

_____

_____

Reflect on your children's accomplishments. What are some of the milestones you witnessed and celebrated in your children's lives?

_____

_____

_____

_____

_____

_____

_____

_____

_____

_____

How did your life change once your children left home? Did you continue to do the same activities, or did you start new ones?

_____

_____

_____

_____

_____

_____

_____

_____

_____

Overcoming a fear is a big milestone. Reflect on an achievement you made when you overcame a fear.

_____

_____

_____

_____

_____

_____

_____

_____

_____

_____

Think back to the biggest milestones in your life so far. What were they? A new job, having children, learning to play an instrument as an adult, or something else?

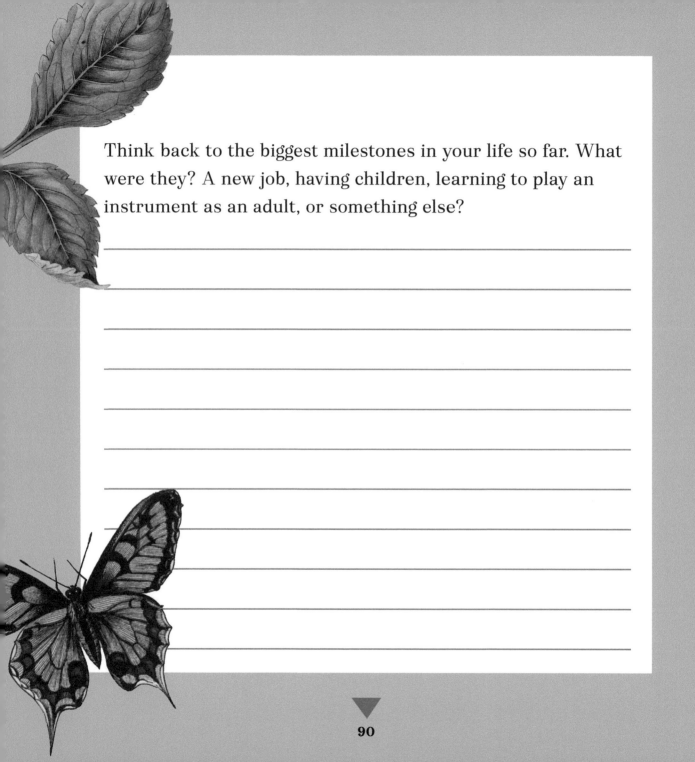

The best way to treat obstacles is to use them as stepping-stones. **LAUGH** at them, **TREAD** on them, and let them **LEAD YOU TO SOMETHING BETTER.**

ENID BLYTON

BECOMING A GRANDMOTHER

What was it like becoming a grandmother? Describe your feelings as you anticipated the birth of your first grandchild.

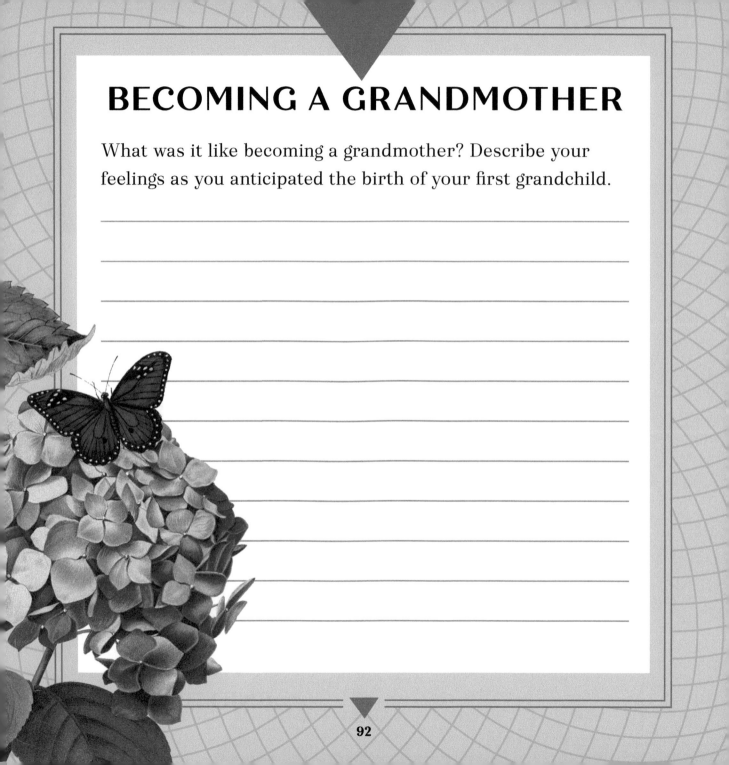

How was the news you were to become a grandmother shared with you? Who shared it? Where were you when you received the news?

_____

_____

_____

_____

_____

_____

_____

_____

_____

Each grandchild has their own personality. Share a special quality about each of your grandchildren that is unique to them.

_____

_____

_____

_____

_____

_____

_____

_____

_____

What do your grandchildren call you? It may or
may not be a traditional name. Share the story
behind your "grandmother name."

_____

_____

_____

_____

_____

_____

_____

_____

_____

Watching your grandchildren grow up, what lessons have you learned? What are you still learning from them?

_____

_____

_____

_____

_____

_____

_____

_____

_____

"

I have a role now
that I think becomes me.
I AM A
GRANDMOTHER.

"

GENE TIERNEY

SHARED TRAITS

Personality traits can run in a family. What personality traits or habits do you share with your grandchildren?

_____

_____

_____

_____

_____

_____

_____

_____

_____

Do you share favorite activities with your grandchildren? Perhaps you both like sports or painting? Share any similarities you see.

_____

_____

_____

_____

_____

_____

_____

_____

_____

Do you share any physical traits with your grandchildren, such as hair or eye color? Describe any that you have in common.

_____

_____

_____

_____

_____

_____

_____

_____

_____

_____

What is one thing that has made the family stronger?

_____

_____

_____

_____

_____

_____

_____

_____

_____

_____

Do you share a gift or talent with your grandchildren, such as a gift for music or academics? Describe these shared gifts.

_____

_____

_____

_____

_____

_____

_____

_____

_____

A clever, strong-minded
grandmother is a
POWER IN
HER FAMILY
and immediate circle.

MARY ALSOP KING WADDINGTON

LIFE LESSONS

Life always presents opportunities to learn. Growing up and maturing into the adult you are now, you witnessed world-changing events.

The advent of new inventions and the occurrence of world events have both impacted how you experience or view daily life. Even small events may have created lasting influences and memories. Each one of your experiences has taught you something about yourself and your place in the world.

The last section of this book is designed to help you reflect on the lessons you learned as you matured and grew into adulthood. You will be asked to reflect on your hopes and dreams and the things you witnessed in a frequently changing world. This is an opportunity to remember and share your words of wisdom and what you would like to be known for with your grandchildren.

WITNESSING A CHANGING WORLD

Reflect on a historical event you have witnessed. Describe that event and how it changed your understanding of the world.

_____

_____

_____

_____

_____

_____

_____

_____

_____

_____

_____

Share a hardship you have experienced. How did you overcome it, and what was its lasting impact?

_____

_____

_____

_____

_____

_____

_____

_____

_____

_____

What invention or innovation has made a lasting impact on your life? Describe how it influenced you.

_____

_____

_____

_____

_____

_____

_____

_____

_____

What would you like future generations to know about the world you grew up in?

_____

_____

_____

_____

_____

_____

_____

_____

_____

_____

What change would you like to see take place in the world for the betterment of your grandchildren and future generations?

_____

_____

_____

_____

_____

_____

_____

_____

They say I'm old-fashioned,
and live in the past,
but sometimes I think
PROGRESS PROGRESSES TOO FAST!

DR. SEUSS

HOPES & DREAMS

As a child or young adult, what did you dream about doing with your life? Did your dreams become a reality?

What dreams or achievements did you pursue that
you are most proud of? Why do these experiences hold
a special place in your heart?

_____

_____

_____

_____

_____

_____

_____

_____

_____

_____

What goals do you still wish to achieve? Share why you have not accomplished them–yet.

_____

_____

_____

_____

_____

_____

_____

_____

_____

_____

_____

You've seen a number of transformations in your community and the greater world. What changes do you hope to see in the future, and how do you think they will affect your community?

_____

_____

_____

_____

_____

_____

_____

_____

As you consider the current world, what do you dream the world will look like for your grandchildren and great-grandchildren?

_____

_____

_____

_____

_____

_____

_____

_____

The future belongs
to those who believe in the
BEAUTY OF
THEIR DREAMS.

ELEANOR ROOSEVELT

WORDS OF WISDOM

What do you consider to be the most important value for your grandchildren to carry with them into the future?

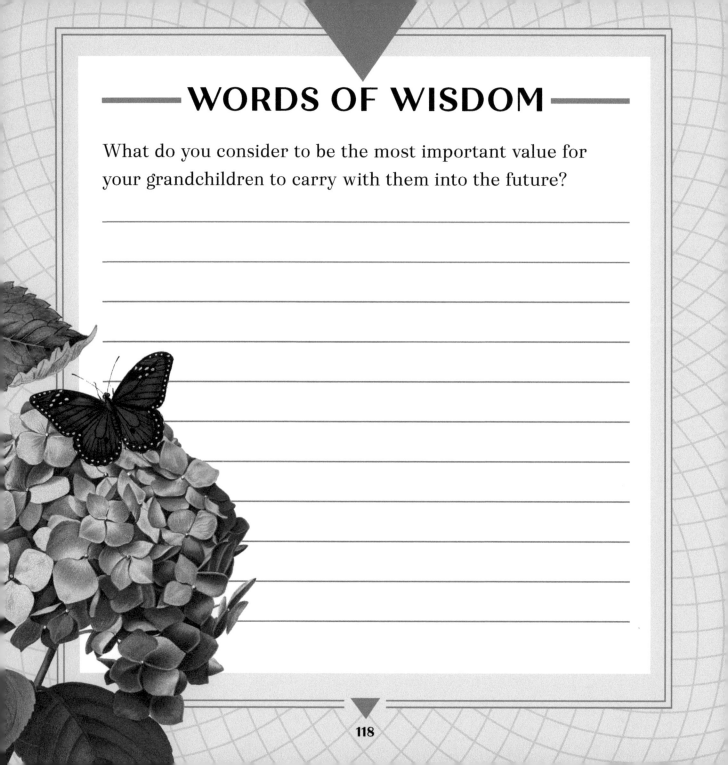

What is the one piece of advice you want your
grandchildren to remember?

_____

_____

_____

_____

_____

_____

_____

_____

_____

_____

What do you think is important for young people to know to become a supportive and loving partner or spouse?

_____

_____

_____

_____

_____

_____

_____

_____

_____

What do you feel is the key to being a loving and caring parent? Pass along your sage advice.

_____

_____

_____

_____

_____

_____

_____

_____

_____

Reflecting on your work life, what did you learn about choosing a career, and what advice would you give to others about these choices?

_____

_____

_____

_____

_____

_____

_____

_____

_____

WHEN SHE SMILES,

the lines in her face become epic narratives that trace the **STORIES OF GENERATIONS** that no book can replace.

CURTIS TYRONE JONES

MY LEGACY

How do you want to be remembered by your grandchildren? What would you like them to share about you with their grandchildren?

_____

_____

_____

_____

_____

_____

_____

_____

Do you have any regrets? If so, what has their impact on your life been?

_____

_____

_____

_____

_____

_____

_____

_____

_____

People are lifelong learners. What do you consider the most valuable lesson you have learned in your lifetime?

_____

_____

_____

_____

_____

_____

_____

_____

_____

What is the most memorable moment from your life?
Describe how that experience affected you.

_____

_____

_____

_____

_____

_____

_____

_____

_____

What lesson did you learn from your parents or guardians that you want to pass on to your grandchildren?

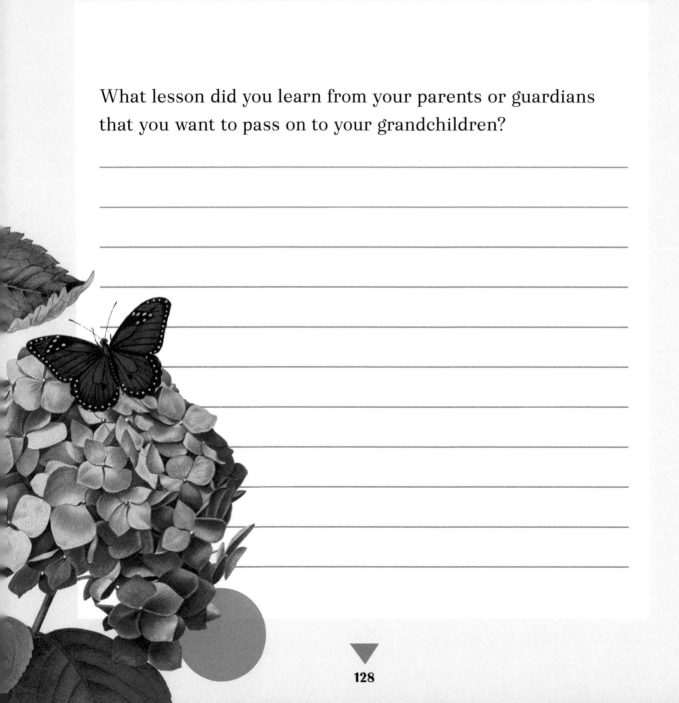

_____

_____

_____

_____

_____

_____

_____

_____

_____

"

Grandmotherhood
initiated me into a world of play,
where all things became
FRESH, ALIVE,
and **HONEST**
again through my
grandchildren's eyes.
Mostly, it retaught me love.

"

SUE MONK KIDD

ACKNOWLEDGMENTS

I would like to thank my many family members who generously shared the family stories that served as my inspiration for each of these prompts.

ABOUT THE AUTHOR

LISA LISSON is a genealogy researcher, national speaker, and the creator of the website *Are You My Cousin?* (LisaLisson.com) and the YouTube channel of the same name.